Yellowfair

Dragan Filipovic

Introduction

He synchronized plate tossing of the Wesselys, a

group of five performers, got a gigantic show of approval as they bowed

furthermore, strolled off the stage. Lee Tung Foo, arguably the first Chinese American in vaudeville, emerged from the stage with the stage empty and positioned himself in front of the predominantly white audience. Lee began to sing,

"Love Me and the World Is Mine," a popular ballad written by Dave Reed Jr. and Ernest R. Ball in 1906. I continue as if in a dream. From reviews and his own writings, we know that Lee performed a comedic monologue, sang a song that was not named in Cantonese, and broke out into an Irish brogue for his rendition of another 1906 hit, William Jerome's "My Irish Molly, O." Lee Tung Foo performed at Keith's Theater in Providence, Rhode Island, and received acclaim throughout the final week of December 1906 and into January 1907, when he sang a drinking song in the original German called "Im Tiefen Keller" (In the Deep Cellar).1 In New England, local critics devoted entire columns to Lee's act because it was original and a direct challenge to American perceptions of the Chinese. Lee, on the other hand, was not Chinese. He combined what he saw in immigrant communities and American caricatures to create an image of what it meant to be Chinese because as an

American of Chinese descent, he only knew what it meant to be Chinese. However, everything was an "act" (see ill. 1). Lee valued novelty, and it helped him draw attention to the contradiction between his ability to imitate non-Asian characters, speak English without an accent, and sing popular songs from the United States and Europe and fixed notions of race. As one pundit expressed, "Not just has he a fantastic voice, which he utilizes with such astounding insight, that one nearly fails to remember his race, yet he sings

what's more, talks easily in English and with an apparent funny bone that is amazing. According to all accounts, audiences were astonished to see a Chinese American perform in American English— something they had to see to believe. For sure, his very presence on the stage tested generally held convictions about entertainers of Chinese drop and proclaimed the rise of scores of

other Chinese American vaudevillians.

1

Ill. 1. Chinese-themed portrait of Lee Tung Foo. Politeness of the California History

Room, California State Library, Sacramento.

An important shift in the relationship between American music and identity occurred when Lee Tung Foo made his debut on the vaudeville stage. His demonstration may

have driven the Provision commentator to "nearly fail to remember [Lee's] race," yet as a matter of fact his

act closely related to race. Musical and theatrical performances about and by Chinese and Chinese Americans had undergone several significant transformations since the nineteenth century. Through the stage and print media, a large number of actors and writers contributed to the dissemination of images of China and its people that eventually hardened into stereotypes. These individuals, who came from a variety of backgrounds, created certain images on the stage and in the music not for the sake of accuracy but rather to assist in defining and comprehending not only themselves but also the people in their immediate environment. A lot of Euro-American writers and musicians made distinctions based on race between music and noise, used racial attitudes to question whether Chinese people could participate in Western music and performance, and then spread negative stereotypes about Chinese people. However, in order to address other issues in the United States, they also turned to China, including gender relations, citizenship definition, working-class identity, modernity's effects, and the creation of novel musical expressions. Chinese and Chinese Americans, on the other hand, had their own reasons for performing on stage. Some were enticed by stories of huge profits and success, but their American managers left them broke. A few Chinese workers, permeated with a pioneering soul, utilized music and theater in order to keep up with their legacy among individual settlers and advancing social comprehension with

pariahs. At long last, the craving of Chinese American vaudevillians, like Lee

Tung Foo, to act in an American famous saying went up against laid out

generalizations by exhibiting that race was a presentation. Even though they have different levels of access to mainstream media, these various voices together shed light on the intricate ways in which race is constructed in the United States and the significant role China played in the formation of American identity and popular culture.

Although a number of historians have examined the connection between African American and Euro-American musical traditions, very few have examined the connections between China and the United States through popular music. Even fewer have looked at musical notation and instrumentation in addition to lyrics and staging. However, the performance of music provides us with a window into the ways in which information traveled throughout the nineteenth and early twentieth centuries and into the perspectives held by various groups regarding the world.

Music is different from written or visual cultural products in that it requires listening. This does not mean that written or visual objects are not used in a historical analysis of music; rather, music must be performed in order to participate in the construction and circulation of meaning.

Music cuts in several directions in Introduction 3 due to its ephemeral and sometimes improvisational qualities, depending on the body of the performer, performance strategies, musical notation, instrumentation, and lyrics. In addition, the performativity of music is not one-sided; rather, it functions more like a conversion between consumers and producers (who are made up of two groups that coexist— the songwriters and the performers). In Understanding Popular Culture, John Fiske argues that consumers can only respond to cultural products in a few ways: Because the performers are not always the same as the songwriters, they can also alter the materials they are singing or playing on a musical instrument in ways that fit more with their own ideas. They can also reinforce, partially accept, or completely subvert the meaning created by producers.3 Historians can begin to comprehend the complexity of representation and incorporate China into discussions of American identity and culture by examining all of these sources and their contradictions.

As a type of execution, music showed up in a few sorts of settings.

Even though the phonograph and radio gained popularity at the beginning of the twentieth century, the majority of American audiences listened to music in concert halls, parks, or theaters. Some instruments, like the harmonica and the human voice, were portable, so musicians could sing almost anywhere; Many Americans also practiced their musical skills at home.4 Even silent movies were not silent; mood" music, also known as the soundtrack in movies and television, was played by a pianist or a small orchestra to set the scene and create a certain mood. Musical performances were a popular form of entertainment in the United States during the nineteenth and early twentieth centuries, and as such, they were a potential source of knowledge and communication—though they were certainly not exclusive to "Americans" or the era.

Music's performative qualities came not only from the venues where it was performed (recordings are, after all, performances), but also from the disconnect between music and everyday life. Music still serves as an alternative to what is perceived as "real" (most notably as a form of escapism and as a tool for relaxation) despite the fact that people whistle a tune or turn on the radio or CD player while they are working or relaxing. As Judith Head servant keeps up with in her conversation of theater, crowds and entertainers share a figuring out that what

is going on is an "act" unmistakable from regular exercises and that the entertainer/

entertainer plays taken on a part that isn't his/her "own. "5 Or, to put it another way, and more in line with music, a conversation between two people relies on the spoken word rather than the sung word (imagine a recitative-style board meeting). The act of singing takes place in a different place than what we think of as everyday communication.

Music, on the other hand, can be distinguished from theater as a form of performance because it is primarily defined as a succession of tones or pitches guided by particular values or rules. The ideas that guide music making, like symphonious development and notational frameworks, are significant in understanding the importance behind these sorts of creative works. Even with lyrics, music ultimately relies on sounds to convey meaning— sometimes arranged in patterns but also unplanned. The majority of listeners associate music's meaning with feelings and emotions; However, like other forms of cultural production, music is a component of larger thought systems. Music demonstrates rationality, gender constructions, and national and racial identity.

A "western style of dominating, restructuring, and having authority over" the non-

Western world, according to Edward Said, is what Edward Said calls Orientalism. By the end of the eighteenth century, many European and American writers, realizing that what they saw as the "laws" of music and drama were not the same throughout the world, began systematically to marginalize non-Western traditions. These notions of the "Orient," which include China, function in opposition to whatever symbolized the West. They frequently depict the "sensuality, promise, terror, sublimity, idyllic pleasure, [and] intense energy" of this region of the world. China's performing expressions customs as of now were different, contingent upon district, sort of service or festivity, sex, and class. Following the teachings of Confucius, literati and government officials studied music and played the qin (a zither) for worship, character development, and good governance. In the nineteenth century, a number of regional operas came together to form Beijing Opera. Women performed in court, brothels, and teahouses; Westerners, as with other aspects of Chinese culture, saw and heard something else when blind musicians played in the streets for food or spare change. Acquiring from the language in which the arising

working classes separated themselves from the average workers and laborers,

European and American essayists clouded the variety of customs in China furthermore, depicted Chinese culture, with few special cases, as absent any trace of anything melodic.

Many people came to the conclusion that the Chinese were incapable of comprehending or producing something that Westerners perceived to be more sophisticated—Western music and theater—because of stereotypes about China's inferior culture that were propagated by the majority of writers from Europe and the

United States. Racial mediocrity, upheld by mainstream views and a developing logical writing, was

appeared in culture — both in the creation of particular kinds of creations and

in the questions relating to the degree of Chinese understanding. By the by,

as Homi Bhabha fights in his examination of race-based generalizations, the conviction

that the Chinese couldn't sing and play in a Western design was seen, from one viewpoint, to be fixed and regular, and then again, "irresolute. "8 A couple of European and American evangelists trusted that the Chinese

could be inspired from their present status of debasement through Christianity

Presentation 5

what's more, become their equivalents; Music was one of their attempts to demonstrate this point. Here, a faith in general fraternity, which upheld their converting in nonwhite networks, clashed with organically based bigot

ideas.9

Albeit still attached to what was happening in Europe, nineteenth-century

Americans fostered their own kind of Orientalism in light of American-

Chinese exchange relations, migration, and logical prejudice. According to James Moy, John Kuo Wei Tchen, and Robert G. Lee, these attitudes permeated the highly commercial and frequently spectacle-driven musical and theatrical productions that began to appear during the antebellum period, which, in turn, supported certain kinds of Chinese portrayals.10 Anti-Chinese stereotypes were mostly found in the lyrics and dialogue, the sets, and the "yelled-up" white body, and they did not show up in the areas of musical notation and instrumentation until the Verses and exchange frequently transferred contemporary social and political perspectives that were correspondingly tracked down in papers,

travel stories, verse, and famous fiction. The allure of the exotic, particularly Chinese export goods, brightly colored sets, and luscious fabrics, worked hand in hand with the visual excesses of staged spectacles, which became more elaborate over the course of the nineteenth century as new theatrical technologies emerged. Yellowface, a term utilized essentially during the 20th hundred years to depict the manners by which white entertainers depicted Asians, showed corrupting

pictures of Chinese migrants on the stage — pictures that were likewise showing up

in contemporary political kid's shows and magazine covers. Similarly as with blackface,

which arose during the 1830s as a well known method for caricaturing African Americans,

tongue, cosmetics, act, and costuming involved yellowface; These things made the Chinese body look foreign and inferior when combined.

The blend of these gadgets didn't be guaranteed to make a one-sided

hostile to Chinese picture; In these performances, allure and repulsiveness coexisted. In their analysis of the European bourgeoisie of the nineteenth century, Peter Stallybrass and Allon White argue that "what is socially peripheral is so frequently symbolically central." Besides, "these low

areas, evidently ousted as 'Other,' return as the object of sentimentality, yearning and interest. "11This also appears in the United States in that what was thought to be innately foreign and racially inferior— namely, Chinese immigrants and their cultural practices— not only defined the boundaries of American identity but also served as a location for the desire for things and ideas that had been lost to "progress" or were thought to be outside of traditional social norms. Thus, Chinese and Chinese Americans, and likewise all people of Asian drop, were fundamental to the origination of American culture and the limits of racial

furthermore, public personality.

In comparison to other aspects of performance, musical representations of the Chinese developed at a slower rate, in part due to the widespread dismissal of Chinese music as noise and in part due to the lack of information regarding Chinese music. Chinese musical tokens did not consistently appear in popular music until the latter part of the nineteenth century, with the exception of a few attempts to use gongs and incorporate early transcriptions of Chinese melodies. American songwriters frequently turned to these earlier attempts to embody the "Orient," but they also used transcriptions of Chinese music as more material became available, as well as two quite different but familiar types of musical otherness in the United States—blackface minstrelsy and African American musical traditions. However, composers had been working with musical representations of other parts of the "Orient," particularly Turkey, in ways that reinforced stereotypes of exoticism and difference while also fostering musical experimentation.12

Blackface minstrelsy and African American music hold much more nuanced positions in American culture than the black–white dyad in music, which are further complicated when mixed with Chinese musical tokens. With some modifications to make them more sophisticated and civilized, some cultural elites believed that each was uniquely American and played a role in separating the United States from Europe. Comparative contentions were additionally made for

Local American and European-based society music from Appalachia. However, there were distinct distinctions. African American music, which was also a product of the African American experience in the United States and was a mixture of European and African elements, was frequently a release from the prejudices that blackface embodied.14 With an understanding that both African American music and blackface minstrelsy were tied to markers of racial inferiority, white songwriters applied these traditions to Chinese immigrants. Although blackface was frequently used to address a variety of social and political issues, it co-opted African American melodies However not at all like African Americans, who were considered by some to be a method for separating the U.S. populace

from that of Europe, the Chinese were not viewed as Americans yet as outsiders. However, composers frequently employed the same musical techniques to convey the "nonwhiteness" of both groups. This peculiarity, as well, was filled

with inconsistencies. Songwriters opened the door to the possibility that Chinese immigrants could also claim an American identity by uniting these particular nonwhite groups through music.

The appearance of "real" Chinese bodies, like Lee Tung Foo's at the beginning of the twentieth century, further complicated the American musical landscape by combining musical and theatrical signifiers in ways that could challenge Chinese stereotypes. As verified by Josephine Lee in Performing Asian

America, entertainers of Asian plunge "rob[bed] the generalization of its capacity to substitute for the regular or fundamental being and reveal[ed] it as a social build, the result of explicit verifiable and social conditions. "15 White audiences expected Chinese and Chinese Americans to reaffirm the caricatures that whites had previously produced in print media and on the stage, as they frequently saw yellowface as authentic and true to life. The evenness and cutoff points of generalizations, in any case, had zero control over Chinese and Chinese Americans on

the stage (even the people who reenacted American personifications) since what they

delivered was "stunning" and unmistakable from their "genuine" selves, which should be equivalent to these generalizations. Performance was a way for many Chinese visitors and immigrants to express appreciation for their heritage, challenge racism, and take control of the stage images.

In addition to demonstrating the musical talent of Chinese-American men and women, those who entered vaudeville also demonstrated the fracturing of racial and national boundaries. They tried a variety of tactics on stage, with varying degrees of success, in the hope that anti-Chinese sentiments and audience perceptions of what it meant to be American would be challenged.

This book's loosely chronological chapters focus on how a wide range of writers and performers constantly created and reworked Chinese stereotypes in musical performances in the nineteenth and early twentieth centuries. The common perceptions of Chinese theater and music, as well as the ways songwriters depicted the Chinese at the beginning of the nineteenth century, are discussed in Chapter 1. Most of the time, commentators from Europe and the United States thought that

Chinese music was not musical and wondered if the Chinese could understand Western culture.

The lyrics, dialogue, sets, costumes, and sheet music cover designs of musical productions with Chinese characters or set in China emphasized what was exotic and different about China and the West. The

development of Chinese outsiders as melodic subjects, first in Quite a while during the 1850s and afterward, by 1870, on the public level is tended to in section

2. Blackface minstrelsy, which had previously been used to denigrate African Americans and certain European immigrant groups, was the inspiration for several of these acts. With few exemptions, tunes from this period supported

perspectives that prompted the section of the Chinese Avoidance Act in 1882 by outlining Chinese settlers as racially sub-par and unpatriotic.

The Chinese performers who made their debuts in the United States at dime museums, Chinese theaters, and, by the turn of the century, world expositions are the focus of Chapter 3.

These entertainers and coordinators frequently utilized their melodic and dramatic customs

to keep up with their legacy for worker networks as well as to address

American generalizations of Chinese culture, opening up the

opportunities for elective understandings of their development. However, their actions only served to bolster anti-Chinese attitudes for many white observers. The manners by which

8 Ye l low fac e

writers utilized melodic documentation and instrumentation toward the finish of the nineteenth hundred years to address China is talked about in section 4. The use of Chinese-inspired sounds based on Orientalist operas,

African American music, blackface minstrelsy, and transcriptions of Chinese music also provided American songwriters with a new source of musical inspiration and innovation, despite reinforcing difference and inferiority through the "yelled-up" body and lyrics. By incorporating these melodies into Western musical notation, it also dispelled the notion that Chinese music was merely noise. Part 5 investigates the heterogeneity of Chinese pictures delivered in the US from the mid1880s through the 1920s, a considerable lot of which didn't be guaranteed to advance thoughts

of mediocrity as they had showed up in earlier many years. Chinatowns' charmingness, potential for danger, and exoticism, as well as the enticing sexuality of Chinese women, became central. As of now, African Americans and white

ladies likewise started to imitate the Chinese on the stage, however with their own thought processes that connected with Euro-American originations of race, orientation, and

present day life. At long last, part 6 gives the last word to Chinese and Chinese

American vaudevillians, who, with their appearance on the famous stage, at

least somewhat disturbed the designs of prejudice that were intended to keep them.

In the nineteenth and early twentieth centuries, anti-Chinese stereotypes and the conception of national and racial identity were constantly shifted and reworked thanks to Chinese and Chinese Americans' roles as musical subjects and performers. Musical performances, like other cultural productions, contributed to the development of a meaning system that physically and symbolically marginalized Chinese Americans and Chinese Americans in America. At the same time, the fact that these stereotypes were being performed independently of "reality" made it possible for producers and audiences to give them multiple readings. Specifically, acts created by

Chinese and Chinese Americans challenged generalizations that prohibited them

from the stage (and likewise, American culture and legislative issues) and attempted to

offer other options. For more than a century, this diverse group of people shaped the Chinese musical appearance, reflecting, bolstering, and challenging the American self-perception.

Printed in Great Britain
by Amazon